UNBELIEVABLE
MILITARY AIRCRAFT

by Melissa Abramovitz

Content Consultant
Mitchell A. Yockelson
Adjunct Faculty
US Naval Academy

Core Library

An Imprint of Abdo Publishing
www.abdopublishing.com

www.abdopublishing.com

Published by Abdo Publishing, a division of ABDO, PO Box 398166, Minneapolis, Minnesota 55439. Copyright © 2015 by Abdo Consulting Group, Inc. International copyrights reserved in all countries. No part of this book may be reproduced in any form without written permission from the publisher. Core Library™ is a trademark and logo of Abdo Publishing.

Printed in the United States of America, North Mankato, Minnesota
092014
012015

Cover Photo: Mass Communication Specialist Seaman Apprentice Aaron T. Kiser/ Department of Defense
Interior Photos: Mass Communication Specialist Seaman Apprentice Aaron T. Kiser/Department of Defense, 1; The US Army, 4; Spc. Tia P. Sokimson, 7; Library of Congress, 12, 15; AP Images, 17, 20, 42; US Air Force Archive Photo, 22; Tech. Sgt. Bennie J. Davis III, 25; Master Sgt. Ben Bloker, 29; Jake Melampy, 30; Mass Communication Specialist Seaman Apprentice Scott Youngblood, 32; Staff Sgt Jeremy M. Wilson, 36, 45; Staff Sgt. John Bainter, 39; Master Sgt. Donald R. Allen, 40; US Department of State, 43

Editor: Patrick Donnelly
Series Designer: Becky Daum

Library of Congress Control Number: 2014944223

Cataloging-in-Publication Data
Abramovitz, Melissa.
 Unbelievable military aircraft / Melissa Abramovitz.
   p. cm. -- (Ready for military action)
ISBN 978-1-62403-656-9 (lib. bdg.)
Includes bibliographical references and index.
1. Airplanes, Military--Juvenile literature.   I. Title.
623.74--dc23
                                                          2014944223

CONTENTS

CHAPTER ONE

SECRET AND RISKY

t was just before midnight on May 1, 2011. Two stealth Blackhawk helicopters took off from a US air base in Afghanistan. The mission was top secret. So were the helicopters. Very few people knew these helicopters even existed. The craft had stealth technology to let them sneak past enemy radar. That would allow the elite US Navy SEAL crew on board to remain undetected.

A UH-60 Blackhawk lands at Camp Ramadi in Iraq.

The Stealth Blackhawk

Stealth aircraft have special features that hide them from enemy radar. The paint on the outside soaks up radio waves so the plane won't appear on detectors. The shape is also designed so radar will not bounce off it. In addition, stealth Blackhawks have five or six rotor blades. Most Blackhawks have four blades. More blades allow pilots to slow the rotor speed. The blades are covered in cloth. That makes the helicopters quieter.

The helicopters were code-named Chalk One and Chalk Two. They were headed for Abbottabad, Pakistan. The copters flew low to sneak past Pakistani radar. All seemed to be going well. Then Chalk One dropped down and crashed. It hit a wall surrounding the house where terrorist Osama bin Laden was hiding. Two SEALs sitting by the aircraft's open door almost fell out. But the experienced army pilot made sure they crashed without tumbling. One of the SEALs later told a reporter that the pilot was a hero because he saved their lives.

A soldier surveys the landscape from the door of a Blackhawk helicopter.

At that point the SEALs had to act fast. They had to change the carefully rehearsed plan to capture or kill bin Laden. The original plan was for Chalk One to hover and drop off the SEALs near bin Laden's house. Chalk Two would drop off one team to guard the area. It would then drop off the other team on the home's third floor. From there they could attack from the top down. That plan changed as soon as Chalk One crashed.

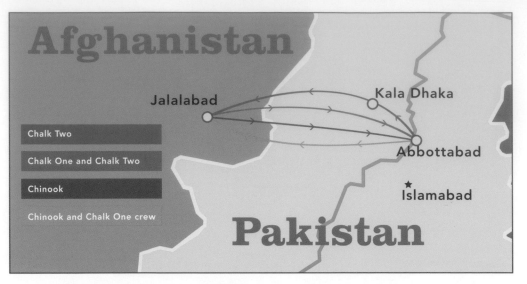

The Blackhawks' Route

This map shows the route traveled by the military aircraft. Chalk One crashed in Abbottabad. A CH-47 Chinook helicopter on standby to support the mission picked up Chalk One's crew and bin Laden's body and flew straight back to Jalalabad. Chalk Two stopped to refuel in Kala Dhaka before returning to Afghanistan. How does seeing the diagram help you better understand the dangers the SEALs faced?

The Raid

Chalk Two dropped off its SEALs outside the wall and took off. The SEALs from Chalk One ran to the door of a small guesthouse next to the main house. They tried to break the door down. Gunfire was coming from inside. The SEALs fired back, and all went quiet. Then they heard the door latch being lifted. The

SEALs wondered if a person with a bomb strapped to his or her body would come through. Instead, a woman with three children opened the door. Her husband, who had shot at the SEALs, was dead. The SEALs subdued the woman. Then they joined the Chalk Two team in the main house.

Together the teams killed bin Laden's son Khalid and two other men who carried automatic assault rifles. Then they found bin Laden lying wounded on the floor upstairs. They killed him after he appeared to reach for a weapon. The SEALs put his body in a body bag. Then they hurried to collect computers and other evidence in the house. They knew Chalk Two was still hovering outside. It would soon run out of fuel.

The Getaway

The SEALs blew up Chalk One because it could not fly. They wanted to be sure other nations could not learn about its stealth technology. Forty minutes after the raid began, some of the SEALs boarded

An Important Mission

The hunt for Osama bin Laden began after al-Qaeda terrorists carried out his plan to attack the United States. The terrorists crashed hijacked airliners into targets on September 11, 2001. Four airplane crashes killed approximately 3,000 people in New York; Washington, DC; and Pennsylvania. In 2011 the Central Intelligence Agency (CIA) finally found bin Laden hiding in Pakistan. The secret SEAL mission followed. The SEALs' names are still kept secret because officials fear revenge by terrorists. This is why a Navy SEAL used a fictional name when he wrote a book about the raid.

Chalk Two. The others boarded a CH-47 Chinook helicopter standing by for emergency help. The escape began. Chalk Two landed in Kala Dhaka, an area near the raid site, to refuel. Then it took off again. Cheering erupted when the SEALs were safely inside Afghanistan.

Despite the crash, the high-tech Blackhawks and the SEALs' quick thinking made the mission a success. The stealth helicopters are one example of the many amazing aircraft that help the US military do its job.

The SEALs didn't want the US military's stealth technology to fall into the wrong hands, so they blew up Chalk One after it crashed. Shortly after the raid, photos of the wreckage showed up on some websites.

> In the days after the raid that killed Osama bin Laden, Pakistan's intelligence service probably allowed Chinese military engineers to examine the wreckage of a stealth American helicopter that crashed during the operation, according to American officials and others familiar with the classified intelligence assessments.
>
> Such cooperation with China would be provocative, providing further evidence of the depths of Pakistan's anger over the bin Laden raid, which was carried out without Pakistan's approval.

Source: Mark Mazzetti. "U.S. Aides Believe China Examined Stealth Copter." New York Times. New York Times, August 14, 2011. Web. Accessed September 11, 2014.

Point of View

Clearly there was interest in the stealth technology of the downed Blackhawk. Do you think the SEALs did the right thing in blowing up Chalk One? Did Pakistan have a right to be upset about not being consulted on the raid of bin Laden's compound? Should Pakistan have allowed experts from other countries to examine the wreckage left behind?

EARLY AIRCRAFT AND MODERN MARVELS

ircraft are an important part of the US military's mission. But military aircraft weren't always as advanced as they are today. The roots of today's high-tech aircraft trace back more than 100 years. Brothers Orville and Wilbur Wright flew the first engine-powered airplane in 1903. The US Army soon realized airplanes could be valuable in war. The Army Signal Corps started an aeronautical division in

Brothers Orville and Wilbur Wright sold the US Army its first military airplane.

War Balloons

Airplanes were not invented until the early 1900s. But some military experts thought airpower could be useful in war long before that. The first air vessels were baskets tied to hot-air balloons. Brothers Joseph-Michel and Jacques-Étienne Montgolfier built the first hot-air balloon in 1783 in France. It was 35 feet (11 m) long. In 1794 France founded the world's first air force. Captain Jean-Marie-Joseph Coutelle and General Antoine Morlot spied on the Austrian army from a balloon. Other armies later used balloons for spying and dropping bombs.

1907. In 1908 the army ordered its first airplane from the Wright brothers. Unfortunately, it crashed on September 17, 1908, during a test flight. The crash killed Lieutenant Thomas Selfridge and injured Orville Wright.

The Wrights built another plane, the Wright Military Flyer. It was ready on August 2, 1909. The US Army purchased it for $30,000. This aircraft was an open-cockpit biplane. This meant it was a plane that had two sets of wings. It could fly approximately 42 miles per hour (68 km/h).

Before airplanes were invented, war balloons were used for surveillance and even bombing.

Many companies started building military airplanes after 1909. Soon pilots were demonstrating how these planes could be used for other purposes. On January 19, 1910, US Army Lieutenant Paul Beck showed that airplanes could be used to bomb ground targets, such as enemy armies. He threw three 2-pound (0.9-kg) sandbags over the side of a biplane approximately 250 feet (76 meters) in the air. Beck aimed for a strip of white canvas on the ground at the Los Angeles Air Show. He missed the target. But later on, crew members learned to aim their bombs.

On August 20, 1910, Lieutenant Jacob Fickel was the first to shoot a gun while flying. He shot a rifle from a biplane, hitting a target in Sheepshead Bay, New York.

Military aviation took a big step forward on November 14, 1910, when the US Navy became involved. That day, pilot Eugene Ely took off in a biplane from the navy cruiser USS *Birmingham*. Ely was also the first to land a plane on a ship on January 18, 1911. Now planes could be carried overseas and take off and land from the safety of US ships.

First Aircraft in Combat

On October 22, 1911, Captain Carlo Piazza of Italy flew the first plane in combat. He spied on Turkish troops in Libya from a Blériot XI during the Italo-Turkish War (1911–1912). The first dogfight, or shooting battle between two aircraft, most likely occurred in 1913 during the Mexican Revolution (1910–1920).

The MB-3A was an open-cockpit biplane used by the US military in the 1920s.

World War I

During World War I (1914–1918) dogfights became common. Pilots who won five or more of these midair battles were known as aces. Most World War I aircraft were biplanes or triplanes with two or three sets of wings and one or two propellers. They were made of wood and canvas. During World War I airplane builders began making planes that served specific purposes. US pilots practiced in trainers such as the JN-4. Bombers such as the Glenn Martin MB-1 were designed to drop bombs.

Some aircraft evolved into multipurpose planes. Scout planes were originally made for spying. But by the end of the war, scout pilots fired guns attached to the front of the plane. Scouts became fighter planes too. Different JN models were the world's first air ambulances, and they were also fighters and bombers.

World War II

Military aircraft had advanced greatly by the time World War II (1939–1945) started. By 1939 most military aircraft were metal monoplanes. These had one set of wings and one to four propellers. They were larger than earlier planes. The larger planes allowed military forces to transport troops and supplies. C-54 Skymasters, for example, could carry 50 soldiers.

In the early 1930s Frank Whittle of England invented the jet engine. Jet engines allowed planes to fly much faster than propeller engines did. The first military jet was the German Me-262 fighter. It could fly 540 miles per hour (870 km/h). The US military soon developed its own jet-powered aircraft. Propellers were on their way to being history.

Military historians believe these innovations helped make World War II the war that proved the importance of airpower. Germany used thousands of fighters and bombers to conquer Holland, France, and other European countries. The Japanese air attack on the US military base at Pearl Harbor, Hawaii,

Ending the War

Airpower was critical in ending World War II. Allied forces attacked Berlin, the German capital, in a series of bombings between 1943 and 1945. Avro Lancasters, B-17 Flying Fortresses, B-24 Liberators, and B-25 Mitchells were some of the planes used. Thousands of citizens fled Berlin because of the air attacks. On the Pacific front, US B-29 bombers *Enola Gay* and *Bockscar* dropped atomic bombs on Japan in August 1945. The bombs devastated the cities of Nagasaki and Hiroshima. More than 100,000 people were killed in the bombings. Many more later died from radiation sickness. Japan surrendered in September, ending the war.

The *Enola Gay* returns from its bombing mission over Hiroshima.

on December 7, 1941, changed history. That attack dragged the United States into the war. And the US military helped win the war with its superior aircraft.

1945 and Beyond

After World War II, a new kind of fighter jet was invented. These jets had triangular wings angled backward. Known as swept-wing jets, their design allowed them to travel much faster than other jets. Thanks to this technology, jets could break the sound barrier. US Air Force pilot Chuck Yeager flew the first supersonic aircraft, the X-1, on October 14, 1947.

At approximately 768 miles per hour (1,240 km/h) the X-1 was faster than the speed of sound.

During the Korean War (1950–1953) the US military added helicopters to its air fleets. Helicopters usually rescued downed pilots or took wounded soldiers to hospitals. Tanker planes that could refuel other planes in midair also debuted around this time. They allowed planes to stay in the air longer. Stealth aircraft originated in the 1970s. Modern aircraft are improved versions of all these types of planes.

EXPLORE ONLINE

Chapter Two focuses on early military aircraft and advances that improved their usefulness in war. The website below also discusses the first military airplane. As you know, every source is different. Read the last paragraph in Peter Jakab's article. What issues does it present that are different from the information in this book? What did you learn from this website?

The World's First Military Airplane
www.mycorelibrary.com/aircraft

CHAPTER THREE

A WINNING TEAM

As modern warfare changed, military aircraft continued to evolve with new technology. On August 2, 1990, Iraqi forces invaded Kuwait, a tiny country in the Middle East. On August 7 the United States and a group of 38 allied nations formed a coalition, or group, to free Kuwait. More than 50 types of modern military aircraft played a huge role in these operations.

US Air Force fighters fly over burning oil fields in Kuwait.

C-5, C-141, and C-130 transport planes, guarded by F-15E fighters, started the largest airlift operation in history. They carried soldiers, weapons, and supplies to the Persian Gulf region. These planes have huge cargo doors. They are big enough to load trucks, helicopters, and battle tanks. The largest air force plane, the C-5, can carry six Apache helicopters at a time. Its four engines are as powerful as 48 railroad locomotives.

US military planes brought more than 482,000 passengers and 513,000 tons (465,000 metric tons) of cargo to the Gulf. That would be like hauling all the people and goods in a large city halfway around the world.

Air Operations in the Gulf

On January 16, 1991, thousands of coalition aircraft prepared to launch from navy ships in the Gulf. Some set off from airfields in the United States as well. Tanker aircraft such as KC-135s and KC-10s refueled other planes in midair. Experts believe tankers were

AWACS Sentry aircraft monitor enemy air and ground movements.

responsible for much of the coalition's success. KC-135s can carry approximately 200,000 pounds (90,000 kg) of fuel for other planes. Fuel flows through a 46-foot (14-m) tube called a boom into other planes' fuel tanks.

Airborne Warning and Control System (AWACS) aircraft such as E-8 JSTARS, E-2 Hawkeyes, and E-3 Sentries took off on January 16. AWACS aircraft informed coalition forces about enemy troop movement on the ground and in the air. Different AWACS aircraft remained in service throughout the war, guarded by F-15E Strike Eagles. The E-8 JSTARS is a modified Boeing 707. Its crew sent air and ground forces information on hundreds of enemy ground vehicles and missile sites. The E-8's radar system can tell the difference between tanks and trucks up to 160 miles (257 km) away.

Whereas E-8s tracked ground traffic, US Navy E-2s and Air Force E-3s monitored the skies. Their rotodomes detected and identified planes and airborne missiles for hundreds of miles around.

The Gulf War

US Apache and Pave Low helicopters fired the war's first shots at approximately 2:30 a.m. on January 17. Their Hellfire missiles destroyed two early-warning radar sites in Baghdad, Iraq. This prevented the Iraqi military from detecting coalition aircraft. Immediately afterward, F-117 Nighthawk stealth bombers dropped the first bombs on Iraqi communications and power centers. Then eight F-15Es destroyed the Iraqi air defense command center.

EF-111 Ravens, EA-6B Prowlers, and EC-130H Compass Call electronic radar-jamming aircraft swooped in. F-4G Wild Weasels began destroying these remaining radars with HARM missiles. Then, B-52 bombers launched AGM-86C missiles at airfields and communications centers.

They destroyed many Iraqi ships, aircraft, and ground facilities in Iraq and Kuwait. Much of this success was because US and coalition forces had the best mix of fast, tough, stealthy, well-armed planes. These planes had the best computer technology and computer-guided

F-117 Nighthawk

Several Nighthawk stealth features help hide it from enemy radar. Its triangular shape and radar-absorbing skin prevent radar detection. Its tailfins hide exhaust fumes. Its two engines are buried in the fuselage. That prevents heat sensors from finding the plane. Because the Nighthawk can avoid enemy radar, it is very effective for a variety of tasks. The US Air Force retired its F-117s in 2008. The planes are stored in hangars at an air force base. But some experts think the F-117s may be used again.

The Tough Warthog

The A-10 Thunderbolt II, also known as the Warthog, is another key aircraft used in the Gulf War. The Warthog has long, wide wings and a large cockpit dome. It also has two huge engines near its tail. With a top speed of 420 miles per hour (676 km/h), it flies slower than many military aircraft. But Warthogs can do things no other aircraft can do. Warthogs dive low to shoot at enemy battle tanks. Then they dart upward while doing sharp rolls to escape tank fire. Their long, wide wings keep them balanced during these rolls. Warthogs and their pilots are protected by 1,200 pounds (540 kg) of titanium armor. They are designed with backup systems that let them fly on one engine, with half a wing gone, and with one tail fin.

weapons. US aircraft could also outrun and outmaneuver enemy aircraft.

For example, an Iraqi Mirage F-1 started chasing a US EF-111 radar-jamming plane. The Mirage pilot fired a missile. EF-111s do not carry weapons. The EF-111 pilot turned sharply and launched chaff, metallic streamers designed to attract missiles. The EF-111 pilot then sped away faster than the Mirage could go. The EF-111 flew straight downward. The Mirage

The Warthog is a versatile and durable aircraft.

followed. Right before hitting the ground, the EF-111 swooped upward. The Mirage crashed straight into the ground.

A Fast Victory

Coalition aircraft flew more than 110,000 sorties, or air missions, during the war. Nearly 250 F-16 Fighting Falcons flew approximately 13,500 sorties—more than any other type of aircraft. F-16s have served

AIM-120 AMRAAM

AIM-9 Sidewinder

AIM-7 Sparrow

Wing Fuel Tank

Wing Fuel Tank

AIM-7 Sparrow

AIM-120 AMRAAM

AIM-120 AMRAAM

The Amazing F-16

The US military has used F-16 fighter jets since 1979. They are fast and lightweight. They can go two-and-a-half times the speed of sound. Pilots like them because they maneuver easily. When new technologies are invented, new F-16s are updated with these technologies. They now have updated computer systems, satellite navigation, the newest missiles, and other new technologies.

the US military since 1979. Pilots like them because

they are fast and easy to maneuver in air battles.

Other types of airplanes were also important in

the Gulf War. F-117s dropped approximately 2,000

laser-guided bombs with amazing accuracy. The

F-117's targeting system allows pilots to hit targets as small as a door from 25,000 feet (7,620 m) above. A-10 Thunderbolt IIs, nicknamed Warthogs, directed other coalition aircraft and jammed Iraqi radars. They also destroyed hundreds of enemy weapons and vehicles with their powerful cannons and missiles.

By February 28, 1991, Kuwait was free. The US military's aircraft were crucial in winning the Gulf War. After the war ended, President George H. W. Bush said the war proved the importance of airpower.

FURTHER EVIDENCE

The main point of Chapter Three was to show how important airpower was in the Gulf War. What evidence was given to support this point? Visit the website below. Write a few sentences using new information from the website to support this chapter's main point.

The First Gulf War

www.mycorelibrary.com/aircraft

CHAPTER FOUR

MILITARY AIRPLANES IN THE FUTURE

The US military still uses many of the aircraft it used in the Gulf War. But it keeps adding new, improved aircraft that can outrun and outsmart enemy forces. Aircraft played an important role in recent wars in Iraq (2003–2011) and Afghanistan (2001–present). Military experts believe high-tech V-22 Ospreys, B-2 Spirits, F-35 Lightning IIs, and unmanned

A V-22 Osprey takes off from the amphibious assault ship USS Iwo Jima.

drones will all help the United States stay strong in the future.

V-22 Osprey

For many years the US military wanted an aircraft that combined the strengths of a helicopter with those of an airplane. In the mid-1980s the military found such a plane: the V-22 Osprey. It took years of testing to be sure V-22s were safe. The US military has used V-22 tilt-rotor aircraft since 2007. "Tilt-rotor" means the plane's rotors can face upward in helicopter mode. However, they can tilt forward to act as propellers in airplane mode. V-22s can hover and go straight up and down like helicopters. Like airplanes, they can travel long distances quickly. They can fly twice as far and twice as fast as helicopters.

The US Air Force, Navy, and Marine Corps use the V-22 to transport soldiers and supplies. They also use it for Special Forces missions and for search and rescue. The military believes V-22s have already proven their worth. For example, in 2011 two V-22s rescued an F-15E pilot who crashed in Libya. In 2010 Ospreys helped navy and marine teams rescue civilians who were stranded by severe floods in Pakistan.

B-2 Spirit

B-2 Spirit stealth bombers are another type of modern aircraft. The first B-2 flew in 1989. They do not even look like airplanes. B-2s have no body or tail. Instead, the entire aircraft, including the engines, fits into its triangular wings. Engineers found that this shape, plus a special

Ospreys to the Rescue

An F-15E crashed in Libya on March 21, 2011. The crew ejected in midair. Unfortunately, the pilot landed in enemy territory. Barely an hour later, two Harrier fighters left the nearby ship USS *Kearsarge* to clear the way for a rescue. They dropped 500-pound (227 kg) bombs as a warning to enemy forces nearby. Approximately three hours after the crash, two Ospreys from the ship arrived. The F-15E pilot lit signal flares that helped the Osprey crews find him. An Osprey landed, the pilot boarded, and they left 90 seconds later. This type of quick, efficient rescue would have been impossible without the V-22.

The B-2 Spirit stealth bomber

coating that soaks up radio waves, made B-2s virtually invisible to enemy radar. B-2s are very quiet, and their exhaust system conceals any fumes that come out of the back. B-2s also hide by flying at 50,000 feet (15,000 m), or approximately 9.5 miles (15 km).

The aircraft's stealth and carrying capacity allow two B-2s to complete bombing missions that would normally require 32 F-16s, 16 F-15s, and 27 support aircraft. But because each B-2 costs about $2 billion, only 21 were being built.

Unmanned Aircraft

Unmanned Aerial Vehicles (UAVs), or drones, are controlled remotely by pilots on the ground. Crew members' lives are therefore not in danger. The US military used AQM-34 UAVs for spying on and taking pictures of enemy forces during the Vietnam War (1954–1975).

Since then, UAVs such as the Predator have been used for spying, search-and-rescue missions, and launching missiles. In 2011 people began criticizing the US military's use of drone-launched missiles. They claimed drones kill civilians the military does not intend to hit. But the US military plans to use more UAVs in the future because of their success in battle. Researchers are even developing UAVs smaller than a human hand. The military believes they could fly into buildings and photograph enemy activities.

F-35 Lightning II

When it comes to amazing technology, the US Navy, Air Force, and Marine Corps' newest fighter jet, the F-35, has it all. F-35s can act as fighters, bombers, AWACS, and radar-jamming planes, all in one package. Three different F-35 models are

Iraqis Surrender to a Drone

During Operation Desert Storm the crew of the USS *Missouri* launched a Pioneer UAV. Its purpose was to send photographs that would help identify Iraqi forces on Kuwait's Faylaka Island. Immediately after the drone appeared Iraqi soldiers were hit by gunfire. Shortly afterward, a drone from the USS *Wisconsin* approached the island. The Iraqis were so frightened that they frantically waved handkerchiefs, undershirts, and bedsheets to signal their surrender.

custom-made for all kinds of missions. US Air Force F-35As operate from air force bases. Marine pilots use the F-35B to operate in remote places with no runways. The F-35C takes off from and lands on aircraft carriers.

F-35s can streak across the sky at approximately 1,200 miles per hour (1,930 km/h), 50,000 feet (15 km) in the air. F-35s also have advanced electronic sensors that tell pilots about aircraft or weapons above, under, behind, and in front. Pilots' custom-made helmets—the first of their kind—display this information on an electronic

The MQ-9 Reaper, formerly called Predator B, is a UAV used by the US Air Force.

visor. F-35s also have stealth features and can jam enemy radars.

Military experts say F-35s will be useful for the next 30 to 50 years. No one knows what the future after that holds. But the air force believes future aircraft will fight battles and spy from space as well as closer to Earth. They are testing aircraft such as the X-51 Waverider scramjet. It gets power from rocket boosters and special jet engines that mix oxygen from the air with fuel. It also rides the shockwave it creates for extra power. The air force is also testing the X-37B, a UAV that will spy from space.

These F-35A Lightning II fighters from Eglin Air Force Base in Florida are flying to an aerial refueling mission.

The US military has been using aircraft to support its missions almost since the first airplanes appeared in the sky. From spying to bombing, carrying gear, and rescuing troops in danger, these amazing aircraft will continue to be an important part of the military for years to come.

Military commanders are constantly faced with convincing the US Congress to provide taxpayer money for new equipment and training. US Air Force General Mark Welsh III explains why it's important to buy new, improved aircraft:

> The air superiority that America has enjoyed for over 60 years is not an accident, and gaining and maintaining it isn't easy. It requires trained, proficient, ready airmen in a credible, capable fleet of technologically superior aircraft. . . . Our fighter investments have kept us in front of our potential adversaries for decades, and they've kept our ground forces free from attack from other air forces since 1953. We're not going to compromise that record. . . . Since April of 1953, roughly seven million American servicemembers have deployed to combat and contingency operations all over the world. Thousands of them have died as they fought. Not a single one was killed by an enemy aircraft. We intend to keep it that way.

Source: Joe Pappalardo. "PM Interview: Air Force Gen. Mark A. Welsh III." Popular Mechanics. *Popular Mechanics Digital*, April 15, 2014. Web. Accessed August 1, 2014.

Changing Minds

Imagine you are in charge of defense spending. You aren't sure the United States needs new military aircraft. Would Welsh's statement convince you to provide money for new planes? Why or why not?

Colonel Paul Tibbets stands next to the Enola Gay.

The *Enola Gay*

On August 6, 1945, US colonel Paul Tibbets and his crew flew the B-29 Superfortress bomber *Enola Gay* on a top-secret mission. *Enola Gay* was a four-engine propeller plane with a special shielded compartment for a nuclear bomb. They flew from Tinian Island in the Pacific Ocean and dropped an atomic bomb on Hiroshima, Japan. Shock waves from the bomb caused the plane to shake and rattle violently—even though it was 30,000 feet (9,000 m) high. The bomb killed approximately 70,000 people in the area. Thousands more developed radiation poisoning and cancer. However, US leaders believe the bomb saved many lives because it spurred Japanese forces to surrender.

Soviet leader Nikita Khrushchev, left, and US President John F. Kennedy

U-2 Spy Plane Incident

A U-2 spying incident almost started a nuclear war. In the early 1960s the Soviet Union's alliance with Cuba posed a threat to the United States. Cuba is only 90 miles (145 km) from the coast of Florida. The Soviets sent troops and missiles to Cuba. On October 27, 1962, US Air Force pilot Rudolf Anderson was photographing Soviet nuclear missiles in Cuba. A Soviet general ordered troops to shoot down the U-2 plane Anderson was flying in. Anderson was killed. President John F. Kennedy's advisors urged him to retaliate. However, he knew that a nuclear war could kill millions of people. Kennedy and Soviet leader Nikita Krushchev worked out a peaceful agreement. Anderson's death could have touched off a devastating war. Instead he was honored for giving his life at a tense moment in history.

Take a Stand

Chapter Two touches on the bombing of Hiroshima and Nagasaki at the end of World War II. Many people think nuclear weapons should never be used. Do you think US B-29s should have dropped these bombs? Write a short essay giving details and facts that support your opinion.

You Are There

Chapter Three describes the use of airpower in the Gulf War. Imagine that you live in Kuwait. How would you and your family react to bombs falling nearby— even knowing that coalition forces were only targeting Iraqi military forces?

Say What?

Learning about military aircraft can mean learning a lot of new vocabulary. Find five words in this book that are new to you. Look them up in a dictionary. Then write five sentences, using one of these vocabulary words in each sentence.

Surprise Me

Chapter Four offers lots of information about amazing new aircraft. What facts about the aircraft surprised you? Write a sentence about what you found surprising about each of these facts.

GLOSSARY

aeronautical
dealing with the science of flight

aviation
having to do with flying

civilian
a nonmilitary person

dogfight
a battle between two aircraft

drone
an unmanned aerial vehicle

eject
jump out of a damaged plane

fuselage
the body of a plane

missile
a weapon launched at a distant target

radar
equipment used to detect distant objects by using radio waves

rotodome
a rotating radar dome mounted on top of an aircraft

rotor blades
spinning blades on a helicopter

stealth
the ability to hide and stay secret

supersonic
faster than the speed of sound, which is about 768 miles per hour (1,236 km/h) at sea level

tilt-rotor aircraft
aircraft that can act like airplanes and helicopters

LEARN MORE

Books

Abramson, Andra Serlin. *Fighter Planes UP CLOSE.* New York: Sterling, 2007.

Gilpin, Daniel. *Modern Military Aircraft.* New York: Marshall Cavendish Benchmark, 2011.

Hamilton, John. *V-22 Osprey.* Minneapolis, MN: Abdo Publishing, 2013.

Websites

To learn more about the US military and its resources, visit **booklinks.abdopublishing.com.** These links are routinely monitored and updated to provide the most current information available.

Visit **www.mycorelibrary.com** for free additional tools for teachers and students.

INDEX

ABOUT THE AUTHOR

Melissa Abramovitz is the author of hundreds of magazine articles, more than 40 educational books, a book for writers, and several children's picture books. She is a graduate of the University of California, San Diego.